START-UP▲
SLIDE GUITAR

It's never been easier to start playing slide guitar!

Published by
Wise Publications
14-15 Berners Street, London W1T 3LJ, UK.

Exclusive Distributors:
Music Sales Limited
Distribution Centre, Newmarket Road, Bury St Edmunds, Suffolk IP33 3YB, UK.
Music Sales Pty Limited
20 Resolution Drive, Caringbah, NSW 2229, Australia.

Order No. AM1002947
ISBN: 978-1-84938-985-3
This book © Copyright 2011 Wise Publications, a division of Music Sales Limited.

Adapted by David Harrison from an original book by Mark Hanson.
Produced by shedwork.com
Design by Fresh Lemon.
Photography by Matthew Ward.
Model: Sagat Guirey.
Edited by Tom Farncombe.
Printed in the EU.

With thanks to the City Lit, London.

Your Guarantee of Quality
As publishers, we strive to produce every book to the highest commercial standards.
This book has been carefully designed to minimise awkward page turns and to make playing
from it a real pleasure. Particular care has been given to specifying acid-free, neutral-sized
paper made from pulps which have not been elemental chlorine bleached. This pulp is from
farmed sustainable forests and was produced with special regard for the environment.
Throughout, the printing and binding have been planned to ensure a sturdy, attractive
publication which should give years of enjoyment. If your copy fails to meet our high standards,
please inform us and we will gladly replace it.

www.musicsales.com

WISE PUBLICATIONS
part of The Music Sales Group
London / New York / Paris / Sydney / Copenhagen / Berlin / Madrid / Hong Kong / Tokyo

Many guitarists dream of playing with the emotional power achieved by the great vocalists.

The human voice is the greatest and most effective musical instrument— in its ability to portray the gamut of emotions, it out-distances all human-made instruments.

Projecting the expressive range of the human voice through the guitar isn't easy, however. The guitar is limited to its neatly delineated half-step portions, which are determined by its frets. These metal barriers prevent the guitar from imitating the scoops, swoops and cries of the human voice.

However, using a slide, the limitations of the frets can be overcome. With it a player can create a range of sliding and vibrato effects, expanding the expressive power of the guitar to imitate vocal styles.

❝ As he played, he pressed a knife on the strings of the guitar in a manner popularised by Hawaiian guitarists who used steel bars. The effect was unforgettable. ❞

Blues legend W.C. Handy recounts his first experience of hearing a slide guitar player in Tutwiler, Mississippi.

USING THIS BOOK

This book introduces you to the basic techniques common to all slide guitar styles.

There is a wide range of styles that use a slide, from the Mississippi Delta blues finger picking of Robert Johnson and Son House, through the more modern finger picking à la Leo Kottke and the flat picking electric lead guitar styles of Eric Clapton and Duane Allman.

We'll start with a careful examination of hand positions for the slide, and then we'll take a look at the three main tunings slide players use:

All of these styles share key techniques and a way of visualising the fretboard. By learning the fundamental skills, you will develop a good, accurate sound with a slide, regardless of whether you're playing on an acoustic or electric guitar.

By studying visualisation methods, you will learn to play anywhere on the guitar neck without getting lost.

You'll find the exercises in this book are written in tablature, and if you're not familiar with tab, a guide is provided on pages 9–11.

Standard Tuning

The familiar tuning of **E A D G B E** that's in general use in classical, rock, folk and pop styles, has its place in slide guitar too.

The fact that you are already used to this tuning is one good reason to try it out with the slide. But as we'll see, it has its limitations, too. Many slide players prefer to play in one of the common open tunings (below).

If you have a guitar especially set up for slide, you can afford to experiment with different tunings without it impacting on your non-slide work.

Open G Tuning

If you haven't played using an open tuning before, you're in for a treat. In Open G, tuned **D G D G B D**, the guitar plays a six-string chord of G without having to fret any strings.

This means that simply barring across the fingerboard at any fret will also create a six-string chord, making it ideal for slide guitar. In practice, you'll often only play a few strings together at any one time in *partial* chord shapes, but these chord fragments are very easy to locate.

And it's worth mentioning that three of the strings in Open G are tuned just as they are in standard tuning. So it's not going to be as unfamiliar as you might think...

Open D Tuning

Like Open G, the six open strings are tuned to a major chord. As the name suggests, however, this time the chord is D.

With the guitar tuned **D A D F♯ A D**, you'll easily locate major chords and a host of others, too.

Whereas in Open G tuning, the sixth string (D) is the fifth of the G chord, in Open D the sixth string (D) is the root of the open D chord, making it extremely practical.

SETTING UP YOUR GUITAR

When playing slide, it's a good idea to set up your guitar strings somewhat higher than usual. This helps prevent the slide from banging on the fretwires as you slide up and down the neck. If the action is too low, you will have difficulty getting a good tone.

If you have an adjustable bridge (as some electric guitars do) you can raise the action, by moving the bridge up little by little until you get a good tone without hitting the frets with the slide.

If you don't have an adjustable bridge, you can try several options:

TOP TIP

Some guitarists keep a slide in the case to use for the odd special effect.

However, if you're serious about playing slide, you'll soon appreciate the benefits of having a guitar that's set up just for slide.

1

Set up a spare guitar with high action.

You probably don't want to permanently raise the action on your regular guitar, and a high action will really help your slide technique.

Since, in slide, the strings aren't generally in contact with the fret wires, the quality of the fretboard is less critical than it would be for a standard guitar. You might find that a relatively inexpensive guitar is fine to practise slide techniques—even one that's been deemed unsuitable for regular work on account of its high action, allowing you to have a separate slide guitar for minimum outlay.

2

Install a *nut spacer* (also *nut extender* or *slide nut*).

This fits directly over the regular nut on your guitar neck. It raises the action of the strings, but requires no alteration of your guitar. To install one, loosen the strings of your guitar and place the slide nut over the regular nut. Then put the strings back on. The string tension holds the new nut in place. Follow the instructions opposite.

These simple devices are available through your local music shop. If you can't find one and still need to raise the action, try putting shims under the regular nut. Carefully take out the nut and lift it out of its slot. Then lay some shims in the slot (cardboard matches work well). Reinstall the nut and the strings.

The nut is usually easy to remove. It is held in place by string tension or with a drop of wood glue. If it won't come off easily, hand the job over to a reputable guitar repairer. It won't cost a fortune.

FITTING A NUT SPACER

Begin by loosening the strings of your guitar. This is a slightly tedious job, but it's made a lot easier with a string winder. This simple device is not expensive to buy, and cuts the time and effort of winding strings considerably—and it'll save you from cramp!

Slacken the strings until they are lying very loosely over the nut.

When the strings are loose enough, carefully slide the nut spacer between the strings and the regular nut, guiding the strings over the spacer one at a time as shown.

The strings should be located in the grooves. You might find that they are spaced wider than with a regular nut, but that's fine.

Be sure to orientate the spacer the correct way around, with the wider edge behind the nut; and ensure that it's placed centrally over the nut.

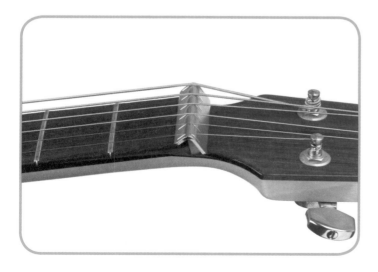

Once the spacer is installed, you can tune the strings up again, being careful not to over-tighten. An electronic tuner will let you know accurately whether you are tuned to the correct pitch or not.

You might find the guitar takes a short while to 'settle', so you'll need to tweak the tuning once or twice.

Now you have a guitar with a nice high action, perfect for slide!

THE SLIDE

Perhaps the most important element of playing a guitar with a slide is tone. Tone is dependent on many aspects, one of which is the type of slide you choose.

The two basic types of slides are glass slides and metal slides.

There is a wide variety of slides that fall within these two categories. Experiment to decide which one is best for you.

Go to your local guitar shop to sample a variety of slides. Eventually you will grow comfortable with a particular slide that best suits your playing style.

If you can afford it, buy several and take them home. You may find that slides of different materials and weights may be more more suited to the different guitars you may have.

For instance, a glass slide may work beautifully on a lightly-strung electric guitar, while a heavy brass or steel slide may work better on an acoustic guitar.

Southern rocker Duane Allman was famous for using a glass Coricidan bottle to play slide. Acoustic fingerpicker Leo Kottke uses a heavy brass slide that is flanged on one end. Blues powerhouse John Hammond uses an 11/16 inch steel socket from a wrench set. Merle Watson used a chrome-plated 5/8 inch socket from Sears. National steel guitarist Bob Brozman uses the neck of a Mateus wine bottle.

Whichever slide you choose, make sure that it is long enough to cover all the strings of your guitar. This is especially important if you play a wide-necked guitar or a 12-string.

Even within the two basic materials, glass and metal, there are plenty of variations.

Plain steel slides are generally chrome-plated, whereas brass or stainless steel ones are normally left bare. The weight of metal slides is appreciable, and many guitarists prefer the very positive sensation of weight on the finger. The impact of the metal on the guitar strings also makes a noise which—since you're not going to be able to suppress it altogether—will become incorporated into your slide guitar sound, so make the most of it. Some guitarists reckon metal slides add attack, or bite, to the notes.

Glass is the material of choice for those keen to replicate the authentic 'bottleneck' sound, since this is where the technique originates. Glass is said to produce a somewhat more refined sound, especially suitable for lighter strings.

Since glass is not especially durable, many 'glass' slides nowadays are in fact made from *Pyrex*, a tempered glass material that is virtually unbreakable.

Pictured here (top to bottom):
Chrome-plated steel; *Pyrex* glass; Raw brass.

HOW TO READ TAB

There are several places on the guitar fretboard that you can play any particular note. This flexibility provides wonderful opportunities for varying tone, but it can be a headache for sightreading standard notation. Tablature eliminates this problem.

Tablature is a musical notation system for stringed instruments that shows the performer exactly where to play each note on the fretboard. This notation is either used instead of, or alongside standard notation, which shows the actual pitches.

If you haven't yet learned to read either system, you should try learning tablature first. It's easier to learn, and it's mandatory for much guitar music, especially for alternate tunings.

The tablature system consists of six horizontal lines, each representing a guitar string. The bass string is the bottom line of the tablature staff, and the treble string is the top line. This layout is inverted from the actual string positions on the instrument. Here, the high-pitched notes lie high on the staff and the low-pitched notes lie low on the staff. In this way tablature resembles standard notation.

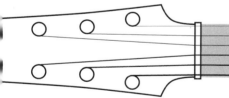

A number on a line indicates at which fret to depress that string. In the context of this book, it means at which fret to place the slide. The following example shows you where to pick the third, second, first and sixth strings, in that order. All the strings are fretted at the 5th fret.

In standard tuning, these notes produce an A minor chord.

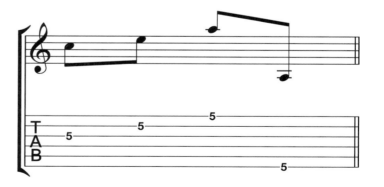

Sometimes, tab includes rhythm stems and beams, just like standard notation. In this example, the rhythm is a series of eighth notes (right).

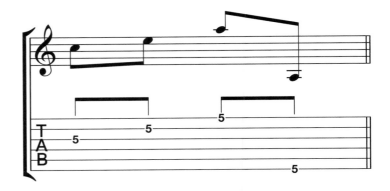

A slide from one fret to another is denoted by a diagonal line between numbers. A diagonal line angling down from left to right indicates a slide descending in pitch (moving towards the peghead of the guitar). Conversely, a diagonal line angling up from left to right indicates a slide is ascending in pitch (moving towards the body of the guitar):

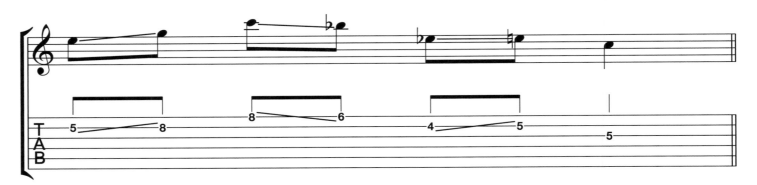

Occasionally a tablature number is preceded by a diagonal line that is not connected to another number. This indicates a slide into the designated fret from an unspecified fret.

Two suggestions about this technique:

1. Unless you want a very dramatic slide sound, don't start too far away from the designated fret. A distance of two or three frets is usually ample.

2. Start sliding on the string just before you pick it. This will guarantee that the initial pitch is not too distinct.

A tablature number may also be *followed* by a slide line. This means to pick the designated note, slide away from it, and lift the slide off the string at some unspecified distance from the original position. Again, a slide of two or three frets is adequate in most instances.

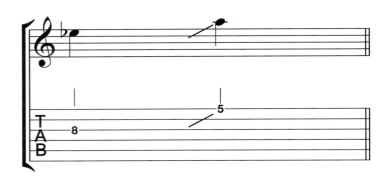

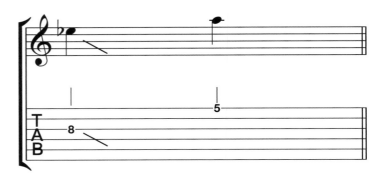

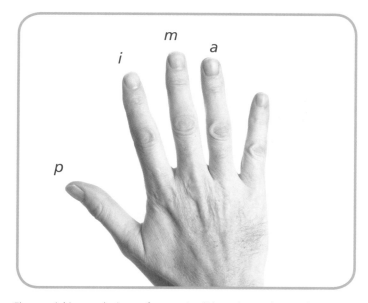

Finger picking techniques feature in slide guitar styles, and usually the picking fingers are named after the traditional classical convention that stretches right back to lute music from the Renaissance.

The '**p**' is for *pulgar*, '**i**' for *indio*, '**m**' is *medio*, and '**a**' is *annular*.

Notice that there's no name for the little finger. Although a name exists ('**c**' for *chiquita*) it's very rarely used, as the little finger generally doesn't get a look in.

Here's how this fingering looks in practice (right):

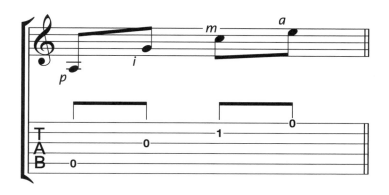

A Word on Slide Notation

In general guitar music, whether in tab or standard 5-line notation, a slide between two notes is shown as a diagonal line with a *slur*, a curved joining line. This indicates a slide acheived by moving a fretting fingertip along a string from one fret to another (right):

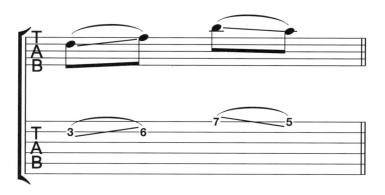

However, in music specific to slide guitar, this slur is unnecessary. The slides shown in this book are all written to be played with a slide mounted on the finger, and are written without a slur (right).

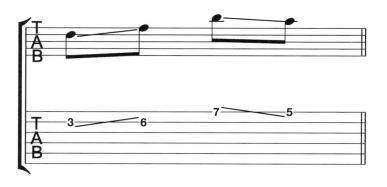

POSITIONING THE SLIDE

There is no set rule for how to place the slide or even how to wear one. But here are some suggestions that you should consider before deciding on your style.

Most slight players wear the slide on the little finger.

Some great side players, however, do very well with the slide on a different finger. Grammy Award winner Bonnie Raitt, for instance, plays wonderful slide guitar with the slide on her middle finger.

Duane Allman wore his slide on his ring finger. Some country blues players are known to have played slide holding a table knife.

> You have to wear the slide on the little finger of your hand. That way your other fingers are available to fret chords. Also, it allows you to damp the strings easily behind the slide.
>
> Leo Kottke

As we'll see, although it might at first feel more 'natural' to have the slide on the middle or ring fingers, there aren't many good reasons not to put it on the little finger.

Mainly, this is down to two factors:

Firstly, the fingers behind the slide are useful in muting the strings, and this helps to keep the sound clean.

Secondly, the little finger is the weakest, smallest and least agile digit. if you find yourself playing slide on a guitar with an action low enough to incorporate some fretted notes into your playing, then it's better to have the three strongest/longest fingers available.

Make it easy on yourself and place the slide on your little finger. It provides for the greatest playing flexibility.

HOLDING THE SLIDE STEADY

Place the slide over the little finger of your left hand.

Then bend your finger slightly so that you are holding the slide in place with the tip of the little finger and the back of the second knuckle.

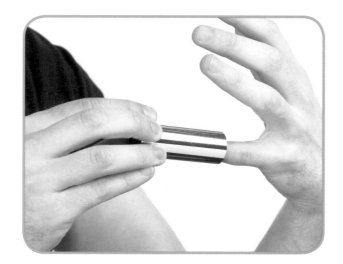

Supply just enough tension to prevent the slide from flying off. This allows you to control the slide at all times. Don't apply too much pressure with the fingers or else you will get tired quickly, and you may produce a cramp.

At the same time, there will be occasions (such as when you want to add vibrato) when you will want to relax the little finger.

LEFT-HAND POSITION

The position of the left hand for slide playing is very important. By 'left' we mean here the hand that isn't doing the picking/strumming.

Obviously, if you play left-handed, then references to the left hand will mean your right hand.

To play slide effectively, your left wrist must be low enough so that the fingers and slide have easy access to the entire fretboard.

The Merle Travis/Chet Atkins-style hand position of the thumb up over the top of the neck won't work for slide playing. A more classical-style hand position is required, with the left thumb about halfway down the back of the neck.

There will be times when the slide will have to lie flat across all six strings. This low-thumb, low-wrist hand position allows you to lay the slide down on the strings very comfortably.

A key to good hand positions is good posture: take care to sit comfortably, but upright and—above all—choose a seat that gives you support and that allows you to keep a straight back, such as the stool pictured. That way, you'll be able to acheive the maximum reach for your hands with the minimum effort.

You'll find you can play for longer and have much more energy to concentrate on the music you're making.

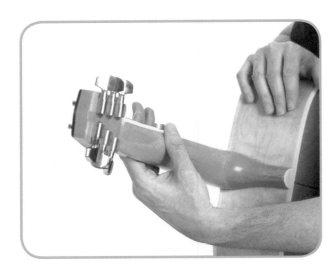

Keep the thumb out of sight, at the back of the guitar neck, for the perfect left-hand position for slide playing.

PLAYING 'ON' THE FRET

You already know that when you fret a regular note on the guitar, you push the string down behind the fretwire.

This allows the string to vibrate from the fret wire to the saddle—located on the bridge—producing a clean, bright sound.

When playing slide, you also want the string to vibrate from the fret wire to the saddle. However, in order to do this, you must place the slide directly over the fret wire.

Because you are trained to place your left-hand fingers behind the fret wire when you play, it will be very tempting to place the slide there, too. Don't do it! The pitch of the note will be out of tune. It will be flat.

To remember this rule, equate positioning the slide to playing harmonics. In order to produce a rich harmonic, you must touch the string directly above certain fret wires (harmonics at the 12th, 7th and 5th fret are the easiest ones to produce). The same is true for the slide. It must be directly over the fret to produce a pitch that is in tune.

If you're used to positioning your finger just behind the fretwire when playing a single note (above) you might need to make a conscious adjustment to place the slide directly over the fretwire (below).

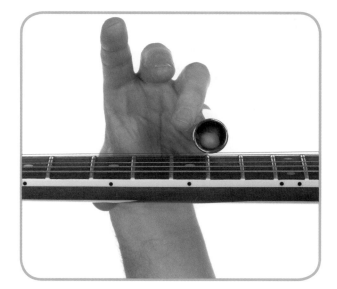

The only time you want to place the slide behind the fret wire is when you scoop or slide it into a pitch. This is very common in slide guitar music, of course.

But when you want to play an exact pitch without a scoop, the slide must be located right over the fret.

THE ANGLE OF THE SLIDE

The slide may be held at different angles to the fretboard, depending on which string or strings you want to play.

If you are laying the slide across all the strings, then it should be held flat, parallel to the frets. You'll soon get a feel for placing the slide exactly parallel to the fret wires and laid flat on the stings. Think of this as a default position.

Later on you will play partial chords; that is, two, three and four strings at once. For these chords, the slide lies flat on the strings. You can avoid striking the other strings in various different ways.

Have the end of the slide reach only as far as the lowest-pitched string that's in the chord...

If you want to play an individual note on a low-pitched string, you might have to tilt the slide so that the very end of it touches the desired string. In this case, angle the base of the slide up and away from the treble strings.

This works only if you have a nicely rounded end on your slide, and the tip of your little finger isn't sticking out of the end.

However, for now, lay the slide flat on the strings whenever you are playing two or more strings.

If you want to play the first (thinnest) string only, angle the end of the slide (the end is near the tip of your little finger) away from the fretboard so that the slide doesn't touch any of the other strings:

...or pluck only the strings to be sounded and mute the unwanted strings of the right hand with the palm:

THE 'TOUCH'

This section assumes your guitar is in standard tuning. Place the slide lightly on the first string (the thinnest string) directly over the third fret. Pick the string with your pick or finger. How does it sound?

Is it like a normal fretted neck? If it does, you may be pressing too hard. Rest the slide lightly on the string. Does it buzz? You might be touching it too softly now.

You must find a happy medium. Don't push the string down so that it touches the fretboard or the fretwire. Apply just enough pressure on the string to produce a strong tone.

When you get a feel for the 'touch'—how hard to push the slide against the string—you will produce a rich singing tone, a tone unlike that of a fretted note.

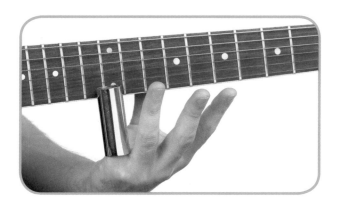

Producing Two Notes from One String

Here's a fun exercise: place your slide at the 12th fret of the first string and pick the string. (Do not touch the string with any left-hand fingers at this point.) As the string is ringing, slide back to the 7th fret of the first string. What happened?

If you have done this correctly, you will have produced two pitches at the same time: one that rose as the slide moved; and one that fell. When you reach the 7th fret, the two pitches are one octave apart.

Why does this happen? If the slide touches the string correctly, the string will vibrate on both sides of the slide.

As you move the slide to the 7th fret, the portion of the string on the peghead side of the slide gets shorter, and so the pitch rises. Conversely, the portion of the string on the body side of the slide gets longer, and so the pitch falls. One string produces two notes at once.

Producing two notes from one string may be fun, but it only sounds good at very specific spots (right on the 12th and 7th frets, for example). Elsewhere, the two pitches together produce a dubious sound at best, especially when the slide is moving. It usually sounds like you're out of tune. This is where left-hand damping comes into play, and that's what we'll look at next.

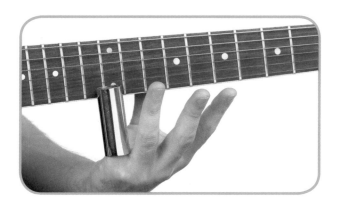

LEFT-HAND DAMPING

If you don't dampen the strings behind the slide (that is, on the peghead side of the slide), the noise caused by the strings vibrating will obscure the notes that you intend to play—the ones between the slide and the bridge of the guitar.

Play the *12th-fret-to-7th-fret* exercise on the first string again. This time, dampen the first string behind the slide.

Place your slide lightly on the first string at the 12th fret. On the peghead side of the slide, touch the string lightly with the tip of the index finger of the left hand.

Don't push the string down; just barely touch it with a very relaxed finger. Make sure that the slide is angled away from the other strings of the guitar.

Take the first string, and then slide from the 12th fret to the 7th fret. Keep the left-hand index finger in contact with the string at all times.

How does it sound this time?

You should hear just one pitch going down from the 12th fret to the 7th. Now try it without the index finger damping the first string, and compare the two.

Touching the string like this stops the vibration behind the slide. You have damped the string. The string will only vibrate from the slide to the bridge, giving you one pitch at a time instead of two.

There will always be some extraneous noise caused by the hard slide contacting a vibrating string. This is simply a fact in slide playing, but you can minimise this by plucking your notes with authority.

Then your desired note will be relatively loud—in comparison to the excess noise.

 Left-hand damping is essential to getting a good sound with the slide.

Leo Kottke

INDEX FINGER POSITION

When you dampen an individual string, bend your index (pointing) finger enough so that the tip of the finger touches the string behind the slide. Make sure the finger is very relaxed. There should be no tension in the finger. It doesn't need to fret the string. It just barely touches it.

Keep your middle and ring fingers close by. Don't let them fly away. If they do, you will have some unnecessary tension in your hand. Relax your hand in order to get the richest tone.

If you lay the slide down flat over a number of strings, damp with the index finger again. This time straighten out your fingers so that it lies flat over the strings.

When you lay the index finger on the strings to damp, keep the tip of your finger in line with the top edge of the slide. For instance, if you are covering only the first two strings with the slide, damp those two strings with the flesh of your finger near the fingertip.

If you are covering more than two strings, extend the index finger along with the slide so that they cover the same strings. Here is the rule: when damping, the tip of the index finger should always be about even with the tip of the slide.

Your left hand should be very relaxed during all of this. If it doesn't, you won't be able to continue for very long. Hand cramps will make you stop.

VIBRATO

Vibrato adds colour to any sustained musical sound, whether it is a human voice, cello, or slide guitar. In many respects, vibrato is the essence of the blues bottleneck guitar sound.

Listen to bluesman Robert Johnson's recordings for a great example of an intense, fast vibrato.

It is tempting to think that the little finger of your left hand produces the vibrato, since it holds the slide. But that's not true. Your whole arm does. Your little finger and the slide are simply along for the ride.

To add vibrato to your sound, your left hand and arm need to be quite relaxed. Place your slide on the first string at the 5th fret. Your left thumb stays in place in the middle of the back of the neck, just behind the 4th fret.

Pivoting from your elbow, move your entire forearm slowly towards the peghead, then back towards the body of the guitar. Your hand should do nothing but hold the slide on the string. As always, keep your thumb in contact with the back of the neck. Pivot on the thumb as well as at the elbow.

Now pick the string as you move back and forth. How does that sound? To get a good vibrato, don't move any more than half a fret away from the original position in either direction. Anything more than that and you'll have a wobble instead of a vibrato.

Practise this back-and-forth motion slowly until you get a feel for it. Gradually speed it up so that it matches the speed of a singer's vibrato. Make the motion concise. Above all, remember to relax!

Once you have your vibrato under control, use it in all of your exercises. Use it especially on notes that sustain more than one beat. The vibrato gives these long notes a singing quality that is pleasant to hear. Long notes without vibrato can sound dull and lifeless.

BEGINNING LICKS

Let's learn an easy lick that is often used by the greatest slide players. The first lick will be in standard tuning.

If you need to refresh your knowledge of tab, read through the guide on page 9.

Place the slide flat on the first two strings at the 7th fret, directly above the fretwire. Pick the second string (F♯) and slide to the 8th fret (G). As the G sustains, pick the first string, also at the 8th fret (C). Make sure you damp these two strings with your left-hand index finger.

This lick, which is in the key of C, is notated below. (If you don't read standard notation or tablature, an explanation is provided in the back of this book.)

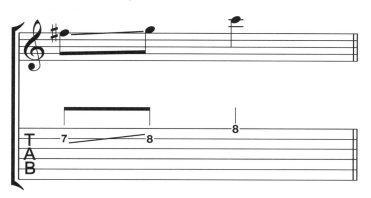

Play it again one octave lower. Lay the slide down flat over four strings, pick the fourth string at the 4th fret, slide to the 5th fret, and pick the third string at the 5th fret. Make sure you are damping with the index finger!

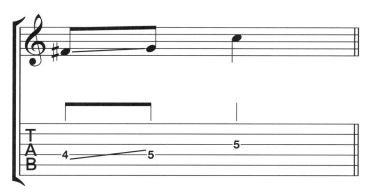

Here's another easy lick similar to the first two. Lay the slide flat over the three treble (top) strings at the 4th fret. Pick the second string, slide to the 5th fret, and then pick the third string.

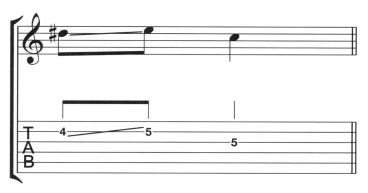

Here's one more: take the third string at the 11th fret, slide to the 12th, and then pick the first string. You should get another C chord.

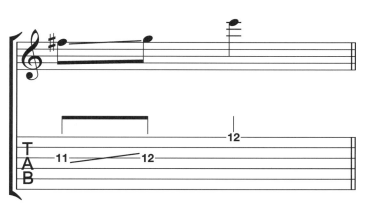

In each of the preceding examples, allow the string you picked initially to ring as you pick the next string. This will produce the chordal sound so characteristic of slide styles.

DAMPING

LIFTING THE SLIDE TO DAMP

Allowing a vibrating string to continue ringing as you pick the next string works nicely when the notes are part of the same chord. But what happens when they aren't?

Here's how to handle this problem. Lay the slide flat over the three treble strings at the 3rd fret. Pick the first string, then slide to the 4th fret and pick the second string. Now slide to the 5th fret and pick the third string.

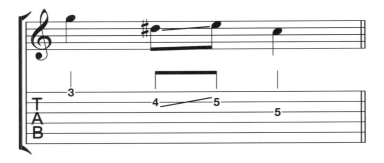

What you're hearing is a C chord (the first string, 3rd fret; the second string, 5th fret—sliding up from the 4th; and the third string, 5th fret).

If you allow the first string to continue ringing as you move to the 4th and 5th frets, you'll produce two errant notes: the 4th and 5th fret of the first string. Neither note belongs in this lick.

How do you get rid of them?

After picking the first-string note at the 3rd fret, simply lift the slide off the strings. Then put it back on just before picking the 4th-fret note on the second string.

Don't lift the slide very high; maybe an eighth of an inch at most will do. You just want to stop the first string from vibrating before going on with the lick.

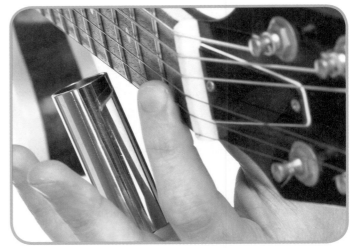

Let's try one more example: with the slide touching the three treble strings at the 12th fret, pick the first string, and then the third. Follow these two notes with the 13th-fret note on the second string. These notes together produce a C chord, but it won't sound right if you don't mute the first and third strings when you move the slide to the 13th fret. Simply lift your slide slightly before moving to the 13th fret.

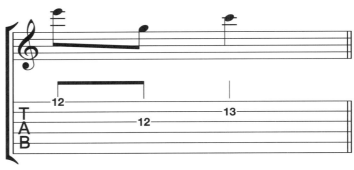

You will probably get a slight noise as you lift the slide off the strings. Be as gentle as you can, and keep damping the strings behind the slide with the index finger. That will minimise the noise.

RIGHT-HAND DAMPING

Right-hand damping is a slightly trickier technique than left-hand damping.

It involves muting a string with a fingertip of the right hand so you don't produce a wrong note as you slide to another fret.

Play the first example from page 22 again. Pick the first string with your middle finger. Next, place your index finger on the second string and pick the 4th-fret note. At the same time, place your middle finger on the first string again—not to pick it, but to mute it.

Now try the other example again. After you have picked the 12th-fret notes, place your right-hand thumb, index and middle fingers on the third, second and first strings, respectively. Move the slide to the 13th fret, but pick the second string only once you get there. This gives you a much better sound than not damping at all.

Very good! You are now well underway to understanding the basics of slide guitar.

PARTIAL CHORDS IN STANDARD TUNING

POSITIONS AND TECHNIQUES

All the examples up till now have been single-note passages that end up sounding like partial chords. To a large degree, this is what slide guitar is all about: a melody moves from string to string, but it often sticks closely to bar-chord positions.

In this section we'll overcome that problem by learning where all of the partial bar chords are (that is, two or more notes) that you can use in standard tuning.

Shown in this section are standard-tuning chord diagrams in the five most common guitar keys: C, D, E, G and A.

Beginning slide players should always hold the slide parallel to the frets. However, this is no good for playing a chord with notes on different frets (as we saw earlier).

Later in the book you will see that playing bar chords with the slide is very easy in Open D and Open G tunings, but it doesn't work as well in standard tuning.

The diagrams show you the most common fingerings for the major and minor chords in each key.

Moreover, they also show clearly which strings within each chord can be played as a bar with the slide.

THE 'ONE-FRET-BELOW' LICK

Take any of the chord diagrams from the following section and apply the following rule to them:

In the slide style, any note of any chord can be approached from one fret below.

Basically you are imitating the scooping of blues vocal styles.

You heard how nicely this worked in many of the previous examples. As you will see later, this rule applies to Open G and Open D tunings as well.

Key of C

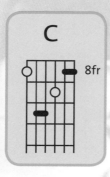 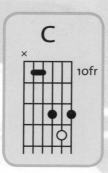 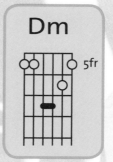 

C   C   C   Dm   Dm

 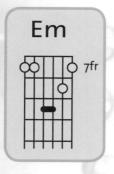 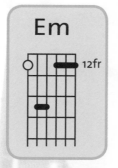 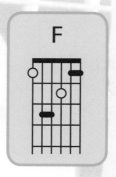 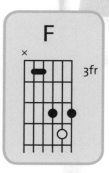

Em   Em   Em   F   F

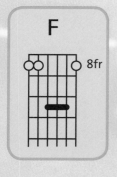 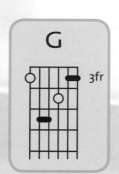 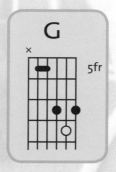  

F   G   G   G   G$^{7\,(9)}$

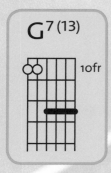  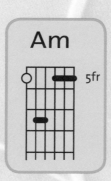

G$^{7\,(13)}$ Am   Am

These common chord diagrams in the key of C show the positions of *all* the notes within each chord. The partial shapes that are most useful for slide guitar are shown in black—and where they're on adjacent strings, they're shown as bars.

Later you'll see that with open tunings, these bars can often be extended across all six strings.

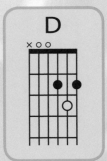 D

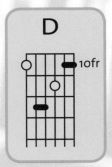 D 5fr

 D 10fr

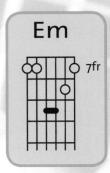 Em

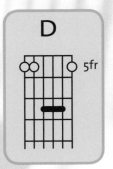 Em 7fr

 Em 12fr

 F#m

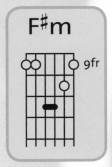 F#m 9fr

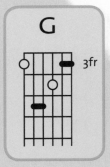 G 3fr

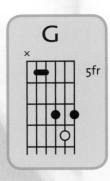 G 5fr

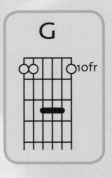 G 10fr

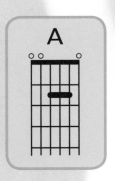 A

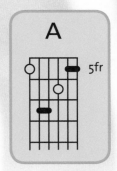 A 5fr

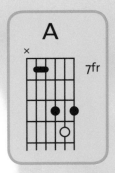 A 7fr

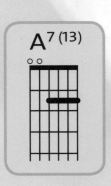 A$^{7(13)}$

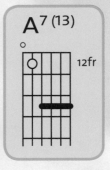 A$^{7(13)}$ 12fr

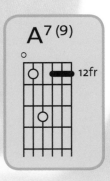 A$^{7(9)}$ 12fr

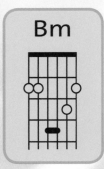 Bm

 Bm 7fr

Key of E

E	E	E	F#m	F#m
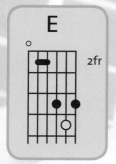 2fr	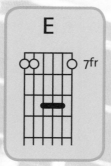 7fr	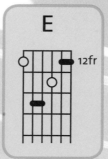 12fr	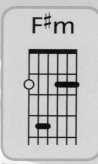	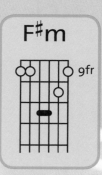 9fr

G#m	G#m	A	A	A
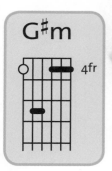 4fr	 11fr		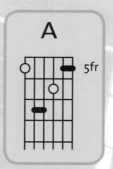 5fr	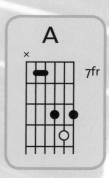 7fr

B	B	B	B⁷⁽⁹⁾	B⁷⁽¹³⁾
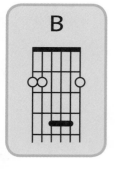	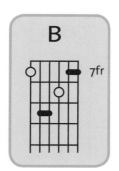 7fr	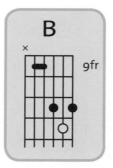 9fr	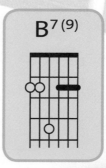	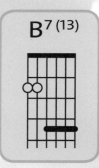

C#m	C#m
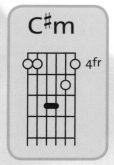 4fr	 9fr

G 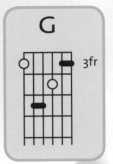 3fr

G 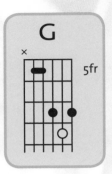 5fr

G  10fr

Am 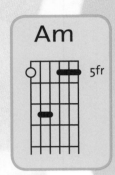

Am  5fr

Bm 

Bm 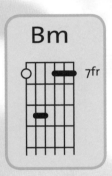 7fr

C 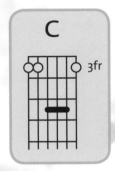 3fr

C 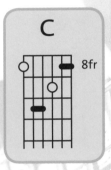 8fr

C 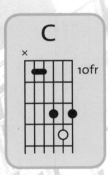 10fr

D 

D 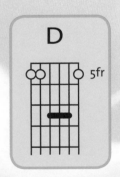 5fr

D 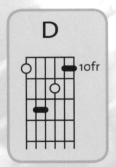 10fr

D⁷⁽⁹⁾ 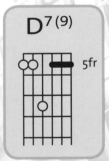 5fr

D⁷⁽¹³⁾ 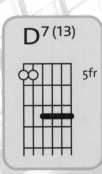 5fr

Em 

Em 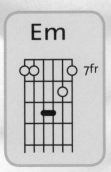 7fr

Em 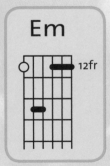 12fr

Key of A

A

A 5fr
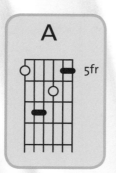

A 7fr

Bm
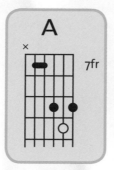

Bm 7fr

C#m 4fr

C#m 9fr
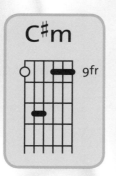

D
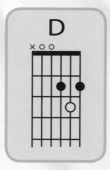

D 5fr
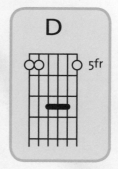

D 10fr
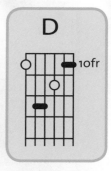

E 2fr
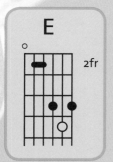

E 7fr
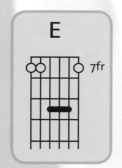

E 12fr
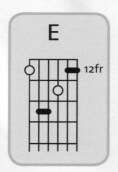

E$^{7\,(9)}$ 7fr
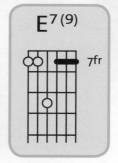

E$^{7\,(13)}$ 7fr
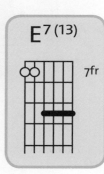

F#m
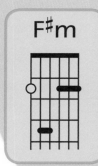

F#m 9fr
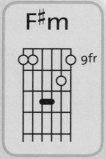

Moving from one position to another within these chords provides melodic movement as you stay close to your chord positions. Shown below are some ideas on how to move from one position to the next.

Make sure that you mute the strings when you change from one fret position to another to fill out a chord. For example, on a C chord, don't let the third string (8th fret) continue to ring as you pick the first and second strings at the 7th fret.

Partial Chords Workout

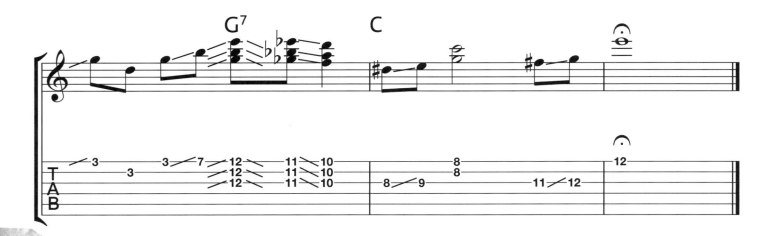

VISUALISING THE FRETBOARD

Good players 'visualise' the fretboard so that they always know what chord they are playing anywhere on the neck (Jazz great Joe Pass is a strong proponent of visualisation).

For many beginning and intermediate players, moving the left-hand up the neck (towards the body of the guitar) is like travelling to a foreign country: we don't know the language. But it is really an easy language to learn. Let's take a closer look:

In standard tuning, you have five basic major-chord fingerings at the end of the neck: E, G, A, C and D. All of the others—F, B♭ and so on— are just variations on these five.

For example, an F chord fingering is really an E chord fingering in front of the bar. A B♭ fingering is an A fingering in front of the bar.

If you look closely at the three treble strings on your normal first-position C and E chords, you will see this same type of relationship (on a C chord, the nut frets the first and third strings for you. On D chord, you need to fret them).

For our purposes in this book, we will simplify this visualisation even more by using only three of the basic chords: E, A and D.

To visualise E, A and D chords up the neck, pretend you have a capo somewhere on the neck and you're playing an E, A or D chord in front of it. For example, with the imaginary capo at the 3rd fret, an E-chord fingering is a G-chord sound. It still looks like an E-chord fingering, but the sound is a G chord because you have shortened the strings.

An A-chord fingering in front of the imaginary capo at the 3rd fret produces a C-chord sound. A D-chord fingering at that position produces an F-chord sound.

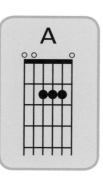

Here are these three chords, named like this: G (E); C (A); F (D). The letter outside the brackets is the sound of the chord. The letter inside is the fingering.

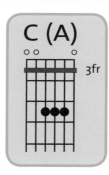

This 'imaginary' capo process works at every fret. But memorising each fingering at each position on the neck takes time.

The examples on the right give you a head start. All of them are C chords. The first example shows an imaginary capo at the 3rd fret, with an A-chord fingering in front of it. The last example is just a D-chord fingering in front of the imaginary capo at the 10th fret. If you memorise the positions of these fingerings, you will be able to play a C chord easily anywhere on the neck.

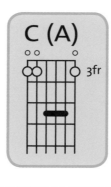
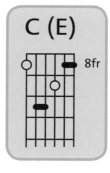

You've probably noticed that these examples correspond to the standard-tuning chart diagram in C shown earlier. Spend some time with all of the other standard-tuning chord diagrams.

You will see that all of the major chords use these three main fingerings: E, A and D.

THE DOMINANT SEVENTH SOUND

A good deal of slide playing is based on the blues. Most blues chords are dominant sevenths. If you don't know music theory, don't worry. A dominant seventh chord is like a major chord but with one extra note. This added note is one whole-step (two frets'-worth) below the root note.

In the blues, slide players move freely between regular major chords and dominant sevenths. The following example depicts this chordal movement around A7, D7 and E7 chords (Play all of the notes with the slide—except for the open strings of course).

Dominant Seventh Workout

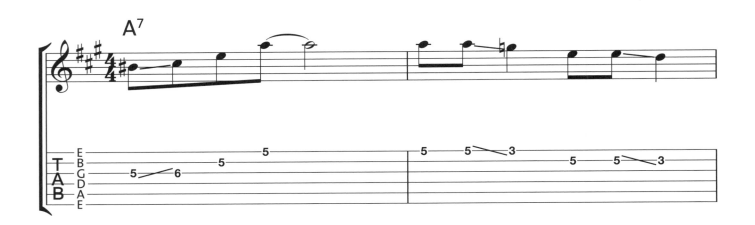

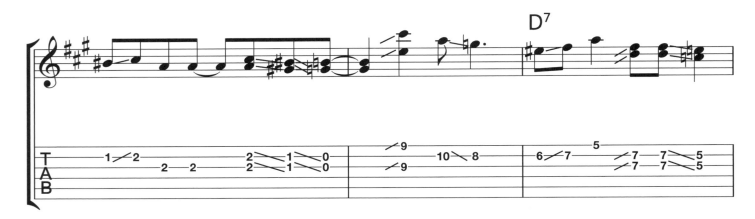

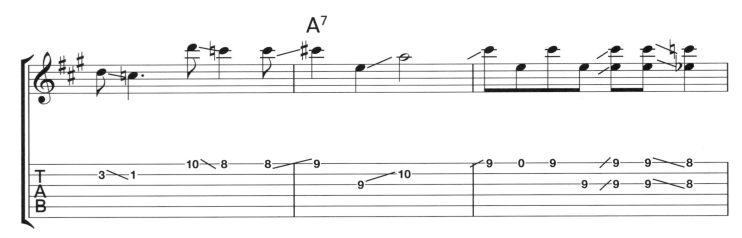

Notice that these melodies use each of the three fingerings—E, A and D—for each chord. Plus, the seventh of the chord is introduced here.

For example, measure 1 is an A chord using an E-chord fingering in front of the imaginary capo. In measure 2, the seventh of the A chord is introduced; it's the 3rd fret of the first string (a whole step below the root note).

Measure 3 is still an A chord, fingered at the 2nd fret. The seventh is introduced on the open third string at the end of measure 3. In measure 4, you'll find the D-chord fingering at the 9th fret—also an A-chord sound. The seventh of chord is introduced as the final note of measure 4: the 8th fret of the second string.

Play the rest of this example and try to recognise where each of the three fingerings (E, A and D) are used. Also, try to figure out where the seventh is for each fingering.

Here's a hint: there are two sevenths in measure 6, one more in measure 9, and another one in measure 10.

USING YOUR LICKS

Try applying the licks in the preceding example to a standard 12-bar blues progression, as shown below.

Make a backing track by recording yourself strumming these chords beforehand, or practise with a friend, so that you can try playing slide licks that match the chords.

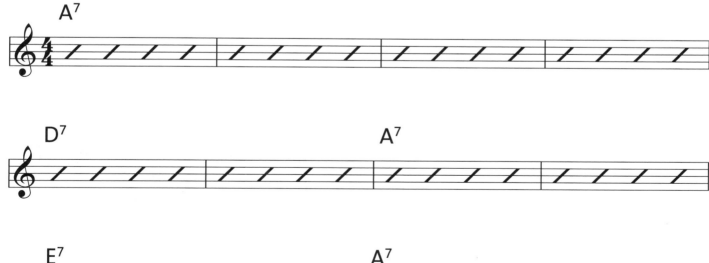

You are now ready to work with the slide in open tunings. The guitar really shines as a solo instrument in these tunings.

In standard tuning, most slide playing lends itself better to the lead guitar variety—playing one-note melodies. You can't play chords of more than two or three strings in standard tuning.

However, in open tunings like Open D and Open G, you can play all six strings at once with the slide and produce a chordal sound. Because the open strings are members of a particular chord, you can play melodies with a slide on one string while the other open strings are still ringing, too.

Playing bar chords on the same fret, and open strings under a melody, are the two basic concepts that finger pickers use when playing slide guitar. Most players—from legendary 1930s bluesman Robert Johnson to modern-day performers such as Leo Kottke and John Fahey—utilise these two advantages of open tuning.

OPEN G TUNING

Don't be intimidated if you haven't used open tunings before. They are quite easy to use. Once you're familiar with them, you'll see how they are tailor-made for slide guitar styles.

Open G is one of the most popular tunings on the guitar. Many of the great blues players use it. It is also popular among contemporary finger stylists.

Here's how to produce open G tuning on your guitar:

- From standard tuning, tune the A string (fifth) down one whole-step to G. The 7th-fret note of the fifth string should now equal the open fourth string;

- Next, tune the E string (sixth) down one whole-step to D. The 5th-fret note of the sixth string should now equal the open fifth string;

- Finally, tune the top E string (first) down one whole-step to D. The third-fret note of the second string should now equal the open first string.

- Don't retune the fourth, third and second strings. They stay at their standard-tuning pitch. Together they already make up a G chord.

- Strum all six open strings together. They should give you a rich, G major sound. If it doesn't sound so good, go back and fine-tune it.

If you still have trouble tuning, consider buying an electronic tuner. For alternative tunings, get a chromatic tuner.

These tuners provide all 12 notes of the chromatic scale, not just the six notes of standard tuning.

CHORDS IN OPEN G TUNING

Here are the positions of bar chords in the key of G using Open G tuning.

Notice how the major chords— G, C and D— are simple bar chords across all six strings.

Since you can't play full minor chords with the slide in this tuning, included are fingerings for full Am, Bm and Em chords. You can fret these chords easily with the index, middle and ring fingers of your left hand. Remember, your slide is on your little finger.

Main Chords in Open G Tuning

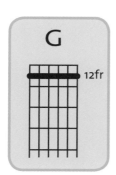

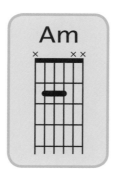

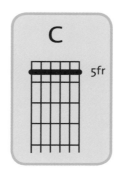

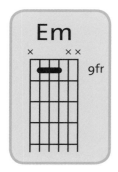

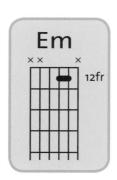

The positions of the major chords that are often used in Open G tuning can be seen overleaf. All but the G, C and D chords are outside the key of G. This shouldn't matter, for you'll hear many of these chords in slide tunes.

The dominant seventh chords associated with these major chords are also shown. Both partial bars (to be played with the slide) and fretted fingerings are shown.

To produce a dominant seventh sound with the slide, simply play the first two strings three frets above its corresponding major chord. For instance, a D major chord is located at the 7th fret. A D7 chord is found at the 10th fret on the two treble strings.

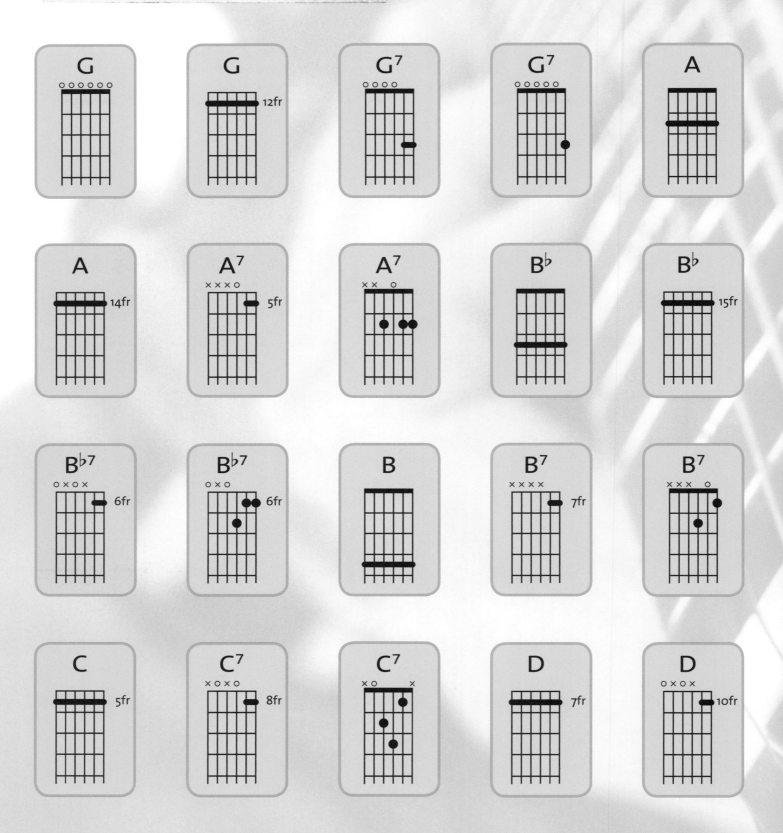

D⁷

3fr

E
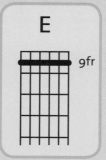
9fr

E⁷
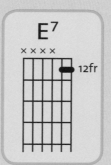
12fr

E⁷

F
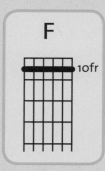
10fr

F⁷

F⁷
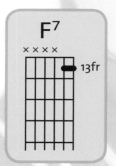
13fr

F⁷
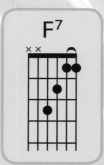

LICKS IN OPEN G TUNING

Here's another 12-bar blues piece, using many common licks in Open G tuning. Since the great slide players use both fretted notes and notes played with the slide, both techniques are incorporated.

The fretted notes, marked by an asterisk (✳), are found in the pickup measure, the next three measures, and measure 5.

Notice the major-chord-to-dominant-seventh movement (up three frets from the major bar chord) in measures 1, 2, 6 and 8. The dominant sevenths really give the piece a blues sound.

There are some open strings in the bass, so finger pick this exercise. Pick the bass notes with your thumb and the treble notes with your fingers.

If you want to play this piece with a pick, play the bass notes with the pick and the treble notes with your middle and ring fingers.

Open G Workout

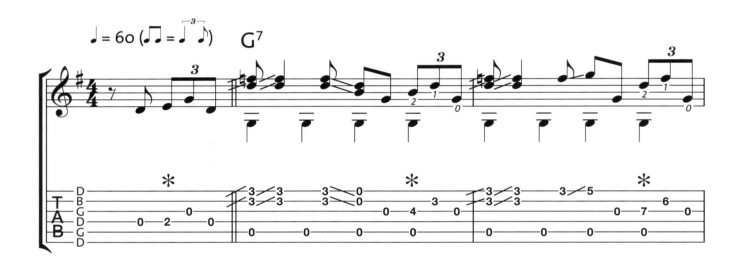

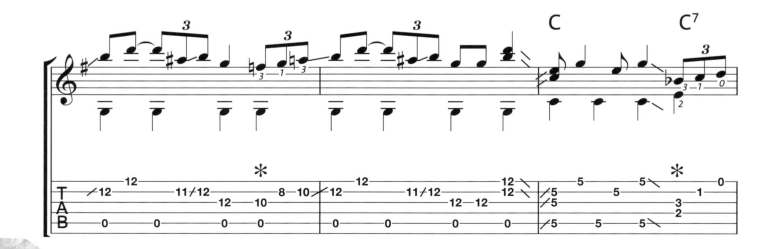

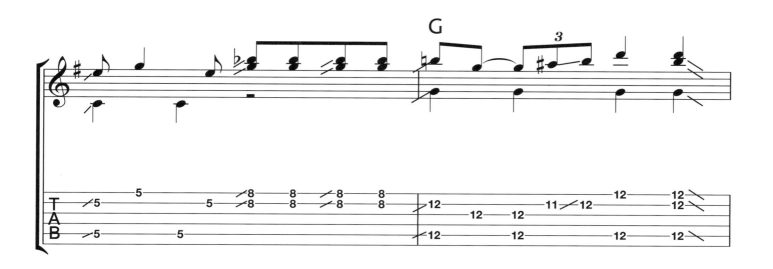

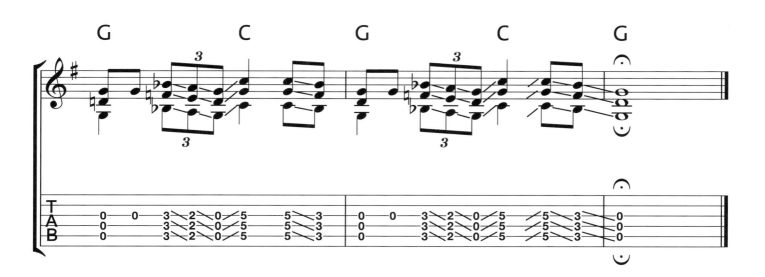

OPEN D TUNING

Open D is the other popular tuning among slide players.

Here's how to produce it on your guitar:

- From standard tuning, tune your first and sixth strings down one whole-step to D, as you did for Open G tuning;

- Next, tune the second string (the B string) down one whole-step to A. The 5th fret of the second string should now equal the open first string;

- Finally, tune the third string (the G) down one half-step to F#. The 3rd-fret note of the third string should now equal the open second string.

One distinctive feature of Open D tuning is that the sixth and fourth strings are an octave apart. This is true in open G, too, but in Open D these two strings are the root of the chord, which makes them especially useful for finger picking patterns. Alternate from the open sixth string to the open fourth with the thumb, like so:

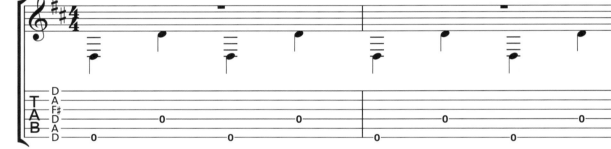

Now add fingers, with accents, to create a syncopated ragtime pattern:

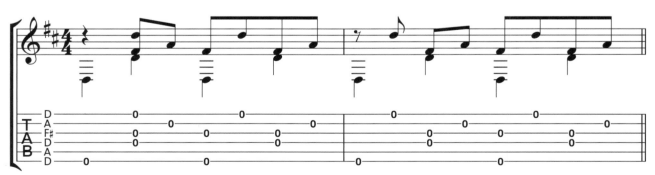

When you're comfortable with this, try alternating to the fifth string instead. Play simple chord progressions with this pattern, moving the slide to the 5th fret for G and the 7th fret for A. It creates a rich picking texture that's just right for slide. Consider compiling your own collection of finger picking patterns.

CHORDS IN OPEN D TUNING

The positions of bar chords in the key of D in Open D tuning are shown below. As with Open G tuning, all of the major chords—D, G and A— are simple bar chords across six strings.

Minor chords in the key of D are also included. You can fret these chords easily with the thumb and index, middle and ring fingers of your left hand.

Main Chords in Open D Tuning

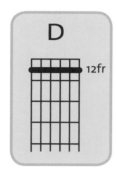

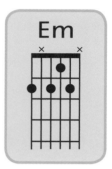

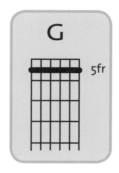

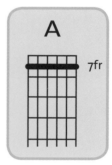

Overleaf are the positions of other major chords that are often used in Open D tuning. All but the D, G and A chord are outside the key of D.

The positions of the dominant seventh chords in Open D tuning are also shown. To produce the dominant sevenths in Open D, play the second and third strings three frets above the major chord position.

In Open G tuning, the first and second strings are played three frets higher to produce the dominant seventh: in Open D, it's the second and third strings.

Try to remember which strings you use for the dominant seventh in each tuning. If you forget, your ears will tell you!

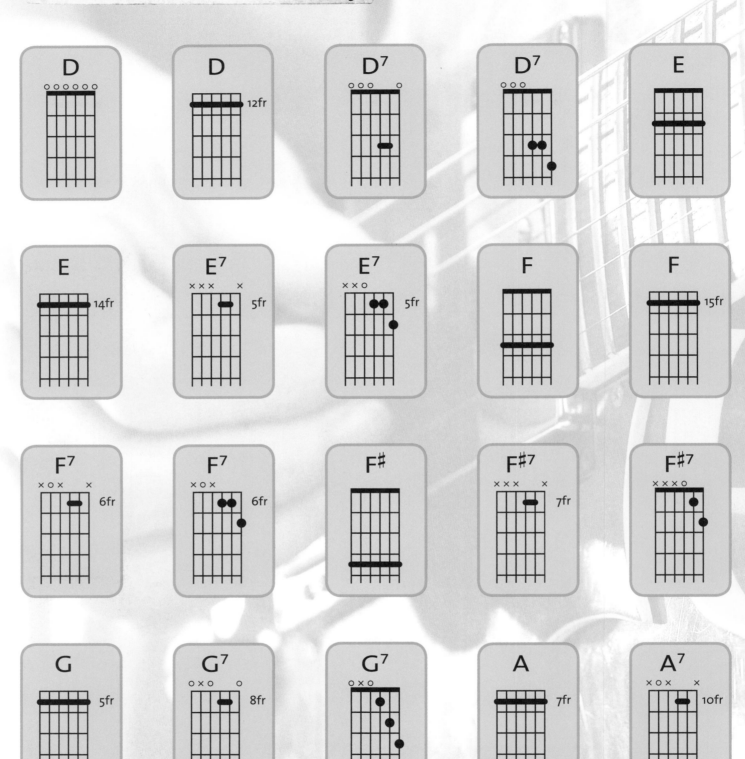

A⁷

B♭

8fr

B♭7

11fr

B♭7

3fr

C
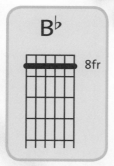
10fr

C⁷

C⁷
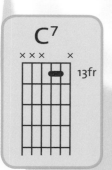
13fr

C⁷

LICKS IN OPEN D TUNING

Open D licks are a lot like those in Open G. They are simply moved over one string.

The relationships of the fifth to first strings in open G tuning are identical to those of the sixth to second strings in open D.

This means that any Open G lick played on the first and second strings can be played at the same frets on the second and third strings in Open D.

When you retune to Open G, try the lick in measure two of the following exercise. Start on the first string and work down to the third string. The lick will then work well in Open G.

In this exercise, a few fretted notes are included in addition to the notes played with the slide. They are marked with asterisks.

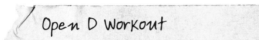

45
Finger-
picking in
Open D

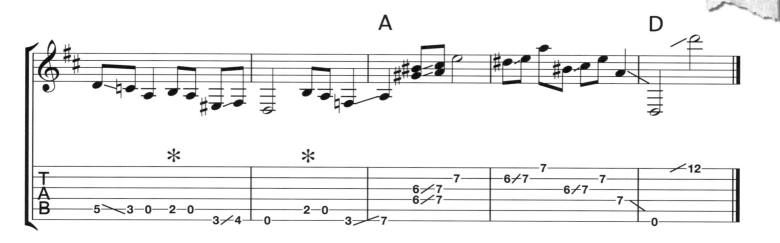

FINGERPICKING SOLO IN OPEN D TUNING

The traditional tune 'Careless Love' (overleaf) is a great slide piece for beginners in Open D tuning. It has an easy melody and uses only three chords.

'Careless Love' has been arranged in the alternating-based style of fingerpicking (called Travis picking, after the great Merle Travis). Your thumb picks the bass notes while your fingers pick the melody notes on the treble strings.

If you have trouble playing this arrangement, omit the melody. Play the chord progression only with one of the two fingerpicking patterns in the examples below.

The first is a simple arpeggio:

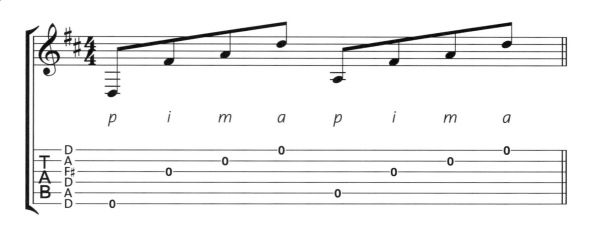

The second is a basic alternating bass pattern that will help you prepare for performing 'Careless Love':

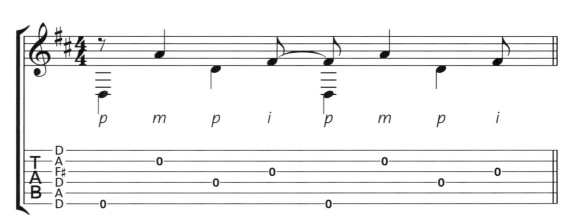

SLIDE GUITAR: WHO'S WHO

Here are some of the great names in slide guitar. The list is by no means exhaustive, but it'll give you a good idea of people to listen out for.

Robert Johnson

Early Delta Blues master. Listen to 'Cross Road Blues', 'Travelling Riverside Blues' and 'Walkin' Blues'.

Muddy Waters

The father of modern Chicago blues, Waters heavily influenced the British blues explosion in the '60s. 'I Feel Like Going Home' and 'I Can't Be Satisfied' are two of his biggest slide hits.

Mississippi John Hurt

Country Blues singer and finger picking guitarist, played slide on such tunes as 'Talking Casey Jones'.

Elmore James

Known as the King of the Slide Guitar. Most famous for 'Dust My Broom', featuring an early and powerful amplified sound.

Bonnie Raitt

Singer-songwriter Raitt's varied career ranges from earthy folk and blues to commercial pop ballads. Check out 'Thing Called Love' for impeccable slide technique.

Duane Allman

With brother Gregg, Duane formed The Allman Brothers Band and in a career cut short at 24, he created the benchmark for rock slide guitar. Listen to 'Games People Play' with King Curtis.

Bob Brozman

A great all-rounder, Brozman is best known for his work wth resonator guitars. 'Rattlesnake Blues' is a great example.

Leo Kottke

This innovative finger picker's influences include blues, folk and jazz. The album *Six and Twelve String Guitar*, featuring 'Busted Bicycle', is a good introduction to his style.

Ry Cooder

Slide great Cooder is known for his collaborative work with many musicians from outside the American tradition. The soundtrack to *Paris, Texas* is perhaps his most famous slide work.

123456789